THE FACTS ABOUT

Interracial Marriages

by Paul Almonte
and Theresa Desmond

CRESTWOOD HOUSE

New York

Maxwell Macmillan Canada
Toronto

Maxwell Macmillan International
New York   Oxford   Singapore   Sydney

LIBRARY OF CONGRESS CATALOGING-IN-PUBLICATION DATA

Almonte, Paul.
The facts about interracial marriages / by Paul Almonte and
Theresa Desmond. — 1st ed.
p.   cm. — (Facts about)
Includes glossary/index.
Summary: Examines interracial marriages and the prejudice and difficulties
that can be connected with them.
ISBN 0-89686-749-8
1. Interracial marriage—United States—Juvenile literature. [1. Interracial
marriage.] I. Desmond, Theresa. II. Title. III. Series: Facts about.
HQ1031.A46   1992
306.84'6—dc20   91-45251

ACKNOWLEDGMENTS:

The Publisher wishes to thank Tamu Aljuwani for review of this project.

PHOTO CREDITS

cover: Bailey Stilleck
Richard Bachmann: pages 4, 8, 11, 13, 14, 17, 24, 26, 28, 34, 36, 39, 41
Linda Harris: pages 30–31
Jeff Greenberg: pages 6, 20

CRESTWOOD HOUSE

Crestwood House   Maxwell Macmillan Canada, Inc.
Macmillan Publishing Company   1200 Eglinton Avenue East
866 Third Avenue   Suite 200
New York, NY 10022   Don Mills, Ontario M3C 3N1

Macmillan Publishing Company is part of the Maxwell Communication Group of Companies.

First edition
Printed in the United States of America

10 9 8 7 6 5 4 3 2 1

CONTENTS

Parents sometimes object when their child chooses to have a relationship with a person from a different ethnic background.

WENDY AND JAMES

Wendy Seever turned the key in the lock and opened the front door. Stepping into the house, she waved at the car that had just dropped her off.

"Wendy, is that you?"

"Yes, Mom," Wendy said, closing the door behind her. She could hear the television in the family room, where her parents were watching a movie. She stood in the vestibule awhile, slowly taking off her coat.

4

Here it comes, she thought. She braced herself for a round of questions from her parents. She knew they were curious about her date. After all, this was her fourth date with James, and she hadn't even introduced him to her parents yet.

But Wendy knew that introducing James would not be a simple exchange of names. It would mean her parents would get to see her new boyfriend. And once they did, they'd know that their white daughter was dating an African American.

Wendy sighed. Why did it have to be a big deal? What did the color of skin matter? But even as Wendy questioned herself, she knew that in the real world— here in her parents' home—it *did* matter. Her father had made it clear. He didn't mind his daughter working with and going to school with people of other races, but there was no way he wanted her dating a man of another race—especially a man with black skin.

Even though Wendy was aware of her father's feelings, she could not understand them. People are individuals first, she thought to herself. What matters is their character and how they treat other people. James was a sensitive, thoughtful and intelligent person, and that was why she liked his company. She felt ashamed about "hiding" James from her parents.

But Wendy also reminded herself that while she was living with her parents, she lived by their rules. If she defied them, the situation might explode. They could forbid her to see James again, or she could be asked to

leave the house. Even though in her heart she felt that dating James was right, living with her decision was not going to be easy.

We've probably heard about situations like the Seevers' before. Movies like *Guess Who's Coming to Dinner?* and the recent *Jungle Fever* have focused on relationships between a black man and a white woman. Books and television shows have also dealt with interracial relationships. Most of us are aware that relationships between races can often lead to strong emotional reactions from families and communities.

But what happens when that relationship leads to marriage?

An interracial relationship usually refers to a union between an African American and a Caucasian—in other words, a black person and a white person. Historically, no other interracial relationship has been the focus of so much discussion and emotion. The history of slavery in the United States has dramatically affected attitudes toward black and white, even today. Of course, relations between other races—white/Hispanic and white/Asian, for example—are also considered interracial. For some couples, an interracial marriage poses the same challenges that any marriage does. They say that race doesn't necessarily create any added tension in the marriage. Some may even feel the differences help to make the relationship stronger.

For others, however, the union of two different races brings up special concerns not faced by other couples.

Any relationship between two people from different ethnic backgrounds is interracial.

7

This book will explore some of the issues involved in a marriage between two different races.

A TROUBLED HISTORY

Relationships between blacks and whites have been happening for a long time. And as long as there have been those relationships, there have been strong negative reactions from communities and lawmakers. In fact,

Laws against interracial marriages were established in the 1600s.

there were laws against marrying someone from another race in Maryland and Virginia in the 1660s. Such laws are called antimiscegenation laws. *Miscegenation* means a mixing of the races. According to these laws, marriage between a white person and a person of any other race was illegal.

But in many cases, marriage was not even the issue. Early interracial relationships were not voluntary. Very often, a white slave owner would take one of his female black slaves as a mistress. As a slave, the woman was forced to comply with the slave owner's wishes. Such a relationship rarely led to marriage. Still, laws against interracial marriage were enacted because of the great fear white people had about mixing the races.

Even after the end of slavery, things did not change much. If anything, the situation was worse. Some white people still continued to consider African Americans inferior to them. African American men who were suspected of trying to date white women were often victims of beatings and lynchings. They were condemned even by those who didn't physically abuse them.

State governments didn't get rid of their antimiscegenation laws. Instead, there was actually an increase in the number of states with anti-intermarriage laws. In 1920, 30 of the 48 states had such laws. The laws differed from state to state. Many said that interracial marriage was a crime. They refused to legally recognize the marriage. Some states had penalties of $1,000 and prison sentences of ten years or more for interracial marriages. Some forbade only marriages of blacks and whites, while others forbade white/Native American and white/Asian marriages as well.

Some laws also included definitions of "black." Most said that having "one-eighth Negro blood" constituted being black. That meant that a person was considered black if he or she had one great-grandparent who was "socially regarded as being of African descent."

The children of white and black relations also had to contend with labels that set them apart from so-called "pure" people. A child of white and black parents was called a *mulatto*.

Children of mulattoes were also labeled by a society that wanted to prejudice them. Those with one-fourth "black blood" were called *quadroons*. Those with one-eighth "black blood" were called *octoroons*. Again, these terms were used both legally and socially to bother and prejudice people. Today, these words are not commonly used because people have become more sensitive to the bias the words often represented.

The *civil rights movement* helped to change some of the attitudes that had brought about antimiscegenation laws. The movement occurred during the 1950s and 1960s. It included protests, the organization of political power and the establishment of new laws to do away with discrimination against African Americans.

The most significant change for interracial relationships happened in 1967. In June of that year, the Supreme Court heard a case called *Loving v. Common-*

In the 1920s interracial couples could be imprisoned. Today, they have the legal right to marry.

wealth of Virginia. The *Loving* case concerned a white bricklayer named Richard Loving who had married Mildred Jeter, a black woman. Interracial marriage was illegal in Virginia, so they got married in Washington, D.C. When they returned from their honeymoon, the sheriff visited their new home in Virginia. They were arrested, tried and sentenced to a year in prison. Richard and Mildred appealed, and their case eventually went to the Supreme Court.

The Court decided that "under our Constitution," the freedom to marry a person of another race resides with the individual and cannot be infringed by the State."

That meant that the antimiscegenation laws that still existed in 16 states, including Virginia, were void.

Today, interracial couples have the legal right to marry. But that doesn't mean that everyone in the United States approves of interracial marriage.

LANCE AND TONYA

Caroline and Joseph Westlake thought they were reasonable, open-minded people. After all, when their 24-year-old son, Lance, brought over his new girlfriend, Tonya, to meet them, they welcomed her into their home. Mr. and Mrs. Westlake treated Tonya as they treated all of Lance's friends. The fact that Tonya was Jamaican American made no difference. "As long as you like her," they said to Lance, "it's okay with us."

Soon, however, the Westlakes began to worry. Lance and Tonya's relationship was getting serious. Lance was hinting to his parents that he planned to ask Tonya to marry him. Though the Westlakes loved Lance—and liked Tonya—they didn't want their son to marry this woman. An interracial marriage, they said, just wouldn't work.

When Lance told his parents of his plans to marry Tonya, the three of them argued long and loud. "We love each other," Lance said. "And we want to get married and start a family."

Lance's parents didn't deny their son's feelings. But they did bring up the issues of society's bigotry, religious and cultural differences, and discrimination. There were many hardships that the couple and their children might face.

"It's not that *we* don't approve of you and Tonya being together," Mrs. Westlake said, "but we're being realistic. If you get married, you're making yourselves targets for all kinds of racial abuse. Have you introduced Tonya to your co-workers? Has she introduced you to hers? Where will you live? Do you want to be stared at in restaurants, yelled at in the streets or even attacked? Do you want your children to have to deal with all of this too?"

Parents of children in interracial relationships often worry that society won't accept the union of two people from different races.

Interracial couples sometimes encounter bigotry and discrimination.

Lance shook his head. "You're making it sound far worse than it is," he responded. "Is it other people who really have a problem with it? Or is it just you?"

The Westlakes are not alone in their feelings of uncertainty. Many people say that though they are not personally opposed to interracial relationships, they fear society in general still discriminates. Like the Westlakes, many people believe that an interracial marriage is acceptable in theory. But they feel that such a marriage faces too many real-life difficulties.

Others say that such an attitude is racially discriminatory in itself. They say the Westlakes are trying to hide their own fears about interracial relationships by blaming society. Although people like the Westlakes claim to be open-minded about matters of race, their discomfort is revealed when something as serious and permanent as marriage is proposed.

The explanations that the Westlakes give—like claiming to have many friends of different racial backgrounds or worrying about the children of a *mixed marriage*—are simply considered smoke screens. They are thrown up to hide the deeper fears about racial mixing that people like the Westlakes might have.

But the Westlakes say that their worries about Lance and Tonya are well founded. Their fears of potential racial abuse are partly based on media reports of race-related violence. The newspapers and television carry accounts of racial attacks, shootings and firebombings. Some people, like the Westlakes, feel that an interracial couple will become easy victims of such racist acts.

CULTURAL ATTITUDES

Despite the changes brought on by the civil rights movement, violent racial abuse occurs today. Legally, interracial couples have the right to marry. And many people have accepted those marriages. But others—both black and white—are still opposed to mixed marriages. For different reasons, these people think that only members of the same race should marry.

In the first part of this century, books were published that claimed that the white race was more talented and intelligent than the black race. These books claimed that any mixing of the races would lead to an upsetting of the "natural order." Mixing would "lower" whites. *The Passing of the Great Race* by Madison Grant was one book that got a lot of attention when it was published in 1916. Grant claimed that it was a scientific fact that whites and blacks were separate species. Whites were the superior species, Grant said. An intermarriage of species would hurt the position of the whites.

The 1920s also saw a revival of racist groups like the *Ku Klux Klan*. The Klan is a group of whites that formed after the Civil War. The group was composed mostly of southern white men. These men were afraid that the end of slavery would lead to the complete disorder of the political, social and economic structures. They felt that all power belonged in the hands of the white man.

In the 1920s, membership in the Klan rose. The Klan was not only antiblack but anti-Semitic and anti-Catholic too. It was, and still is, violently opposed to racial mixing. The Klan still exists today, and it continues to voice its opposition to interracial relationships.

According to a Gallup Poll in 1968, 76 percent of white Americans disapproved of interracial marriage. By 1983, only 50 percent of white Americans disapproved. Some say the change may be due to the civil rights movement and its efforts toward *desegregation*.

Desegregation is a move to stop separating certain racial groups from others. In earlier decades, public facilities were often separated based on color. For example, instead of one drinking fountain to be used by all, two drinking fountains were set up, one labeled "black" and one "white." Schools, buses and public bathrooms were all separated into "black" and "white." Desegregation tried to put an end to this separation, to give equal access to all facilities to all groups. As different racial groups began living and working side by side, some

Despite the changes brought about by the civil rights movement, racial tension still exists today.

people gradually began to get used to the idea of racial mixing.

Many white Americans assumed that people of African ancestry would be in favor of interracial marriage. They felt that a marriage to whites would increase blacks' social status. But many blacks did not agree.

In the 1960s, the black power movement promoted racial pride and strength. Groups like the Black Panthers called for blacks to reject the structures set up by white leadership and "determine our own destiny." And Malcolm X, a black leader, discouraged sexual relationships with whites in his early leadership years as part of that effort to embrace and promote black culture. After decades of being labeled "inferior," many blacks wanted to emphasize the beauty and dignity of their own race by marrying only within that race.

SAME DIFFERENCE

Standing inside the beauty shop, Julia looked out the big front window expectantly. She brushed some pieces of hair from her shirt, then looked up and down the street again. Where is he? she thought.

"Do you want me to call you a cab, Mrs. Evanston?" the receptionist suddenly said behind her.

"No, thank you," Julia said, smiling. "My husband said he'll pick me up on his way from the office." She turned back to the window, in time to see her husband, Roger, getting out of the car across the street. "In fact," she said to the receptionist, "here he is now."

The receptionist looked out the window. "Um, do you mean that black man crossing the street?" the receptionist asked.

"Yes," said Julia, turning to look at the receptionist.

"Oh, don't get me wrong," the receptionist said quickly. "I mean, I think mixed marriages are cool. But it must be really hard, right?"

Julia sighed. "No," she said in a tired voice, as she walked out the door to meet Roger.

As they drove home, Julia thought about the receptionist's question. Why don't people ask *other* couples if marriage is hard? Julia thought. It can be hard for any couple. Every couple has their differences.

But in fact, Julia thought, glancing at Roger, it's those differences that can make it great. Like music, for example. When she and Roger had met, she had hated rap music. And Roger had hated classical. But after listening to some of Roger's favorite rappers—and hearing Roger sing along—she had decided that some of it was pretty good. So good, in fact, that she'd bought a tape of her own.

And she remembered how surprised she'd been when she came home one day to find Roger listening to one of her classical tapes. Mozart soon became a regular in the morning. It was amazing what living in the same house could do, she thought.

It was a lot more than just music too. Julia's favorite meals, for example, came from her grandmother's old French recipes. And Roger loved his mother's southern-style cooking. So now, thought Julia, a whole new world had opened up for each of them. Julia had learned to make real—and really good—southern fried chicken. And, she had to admit, Roger could make a soufflé almost as well as her grandmother.

Of course, some of their differences had been sources of worry for Julia and Roger when they got married. Julia had been raised as a Catholic, while Roger was a Baptist. Although neither of them felt they were deeply religious, neither wanted to abandon the religion they had grown up with. So they didn't. Instead, they attended both Catholic and Baptist services and tried to teach each other about their beliefs. It wasn't a perfect setup, thought Julia. But still, she couldn't imagine *not* hearing about Roger's faith and not meeting his friends at church. It just wouldn't seem natural. Sharing their differences had helped make the differences seem much smaller.

Other interracial couples agree that their differences make their marriages interesting. They believe that they can learn to understand each other better by working through any cultural differences. And, they say, it is understanding, accepting and loving your spouse that helps strengthen any marriage.

Differences in ethnic backgrounds can enrich lives.

"THERE'S NO PLACE LIKE HOME"

Alan Garrett poked his head through the realtor's office door. "Good morning, Barbara," he said cheerfully. "Are you ready for our appointment?"

Barbara Lowe looked up from her desk at the real estate agency. "Hi, there," she said. "Just let me grab my keys, and I'll show you the house of your dreams." She smiled. "Why don't you follow me in your car? Will your wife be with you this time?"

"Yes," Alan said. "She's waiting in the car."

As he followed Barbara's car through neatly kept streets, Alan enthusiastically told his wife, Sheila, about the house they hoped to buy. "Oh, did I tell you about the fireplace?" he asked.

Sheila smiled. "About four times," she said. She could tell that her husband was eager to buy this house.

They walked up the little path leading to the front porch and met Barbara on the porch. Alan introduced his wife to the real estate agent.

"Nice to meet you," said Sheila, holding out her hand. But even as she shook hands with the real estate agent, she could tell that something was wrong. Instead of opening the door to the house, Barbara fumbled with her keys and continued to look at Sheila.

"Well," Alan said, "shall we go in the house?"

Sheila turned quickly to give her husband a silent signal with her eyes. By the look on his face, she knew what was going on—he hadn't told the real estate agent that Sheila was an African-American woman. Sheila turned her face from Barbara and rolled her eyes. Here we go again, she thought.

She and Alan had been looking for a racially mixed neighborhood. But it seemed difficult to find a neighborhood that accepted both of them. Once a real estate agent saw that they were an interracial couple, the agent suddenly wasn't as interested in renting to them.

Barbara paused for a moment and then began speaking very quickly. "You know, Alan, I was thinking on the way over here. I know we thought this house was just what you were looking for, but you know, the more I started to think about it, the more I wondered whether this neighborhood was, well, *right* for you. I know of lots of other houses I could show you, and I'm not sure you'd want to rush into anything here, because, you know, I want you to feel comfortable about where you're living."

Alan stared at Barbara. "I'm not sure I understand," he said to Barbara. "Yesterday this seemed like the perfect house in the perfect neighborhood. If—"

Suddenly Sheila's angry voice cut him off. "Oh, come on, Alan, we don't have to be polite! The only thing that isn't 'right' about this neighborhood is its tired attitude toward color!"

It can be difficult for interracial couples to find a place to live.

"Oh, no!" Barbara said quickly. "Believe me, that has nothing to do with it. It's just that I know you were looking for a quiet block, and I just realized that this block has a lot of small children, and —"

"Yeah, I know," Sheila said in an exasperated voice. "It's always something else. But isn't it funny that we seem to be the only couple that has all these problems?"

The frustration Alan and Sheila are feeling is shared by some other interracial couples. These couples say that while members of the community often deny that racial mixing bothers them, they don't want their own neighborhoods to be racially mixed.

24

Recently, real estate offices that introduce different races to neighborhoods have been firebombed and vandalized. The damage is done by those who do not want other ethnic groups living in their neighborhoods. They fear that the neighborhood, which feels safe and comfortable to them, will somehow change for the worse if "different" people move in.

Such attitudes are quite threatening to interracial couples. Like any married couple, they simply want a home and some peace and quiet there. While housing discrimination is illegal, there are often "subtle" ways to get people out of a neighborhood. Unfriendliness, threats or even physical violence can be used to make an interracial couple feel scared or bothered enough to leave. Couples like Alan and Sheila feel that they aren't able to freely choose where they live, simply because of their race. They may find themselves making a careful search for an established racially mixed neighborhood.

They may also feel pressure from other parts of the community. Some couples have said that their co-workers or supervisors disapprove of their interracial marriage. These couples may not be invited to work-related parties or dinners. Even something like a company picnic can be uncomfortable if other employees are rude or hostile.

Those who openly disapprove of interracial relationships can make life uncomfortable for mixed couples in other ways too. These couples say that they've received poor seating at restaurants, a lack of attention at hospitals and racist comments at school PTA meetings. While such treatment isn't given to every interracial couple every time, many couples say it happens often enough to be bothersome or even threatening.

"WE DON'T WANT YOUR KIND HERE!"

Woody and Charlotte Winchester, an interracial couple who lived in suburban Connecticut, were excited about their upcoming vacation in New York City. Their

While ethnic diversity is commonly accepted in the workplace, many people still believe that interracial marriage is wrong.

plans included staying at a lavish hotel, attending a Broadway play and dining at some of New York's most famous restaurants. This second honeymoon, they thought, would be one they would remember for a lifetime. Unfortunately, the Winchesters would remember the weekend forever, but it would not be a pleasant memory.

The Winchesters' trip started happily enough. A carriage ride through Central Park and a late supper at a fashionable restaurant left the Winchesters tired but enjoying Manhattan's nightlife. Reaching the hotel, the Winchesters decided to check in and have drinks sent up to their room.

Asking for a room, Woody Winchester was met by a tired-looking desk clerk. As the clerk looked at the interracial couple, he said, "I'm sorry, but the hotel is full. We have no rooms left. I'd suggest you look for another hotel, one more suited to your needs."

"What do you mean?" asked Mr. Winchester. "When I called a couple of hours ago, I was told that there were plenty of rooms. My wife and I would like one."

"Your *wife?*" the clerk said, raising an eyebrow. "Yeah, right. Look, I've heard it a thousand times. We don't have rooms for what you want. But there are plenty of hotels around that do. They'll charge you by the hour." The clerk turned away from the Winchesters.

Woody Winchester became enraged. He couldn't believe what he was hearing. The clerk was assuming that his wife was a prostitute! And that they were look-

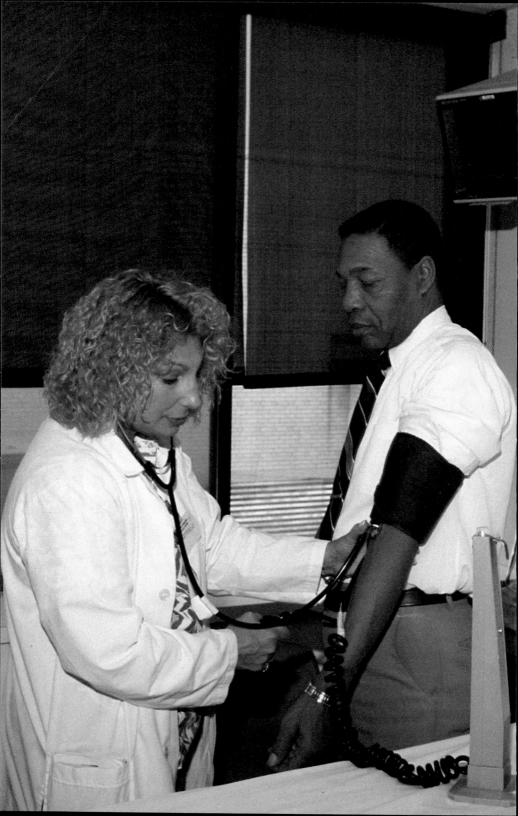

ing for a quick, cheap room! "What right do you have to speak to us like that? Where's your manager?" he said to the clerk, his voice rising.

"C'mon, buddy, give me a break, huh?" the clerk said. "I'm sorry, but we just don't have any rooms."

"Give *you* a break?" Mr. Winchester yelled. "I'm not moving from this spot until you apologize to me and my wife and call your manager."

The clerk hesitated as he looked at the Winchesters' luggage and the credit card Mr. Winchester was holding.

"Look, I—I—I'm sorry," stammered the clerk. "I just didn't think you two would be married. I mean, she's black, and she looks so young. And we do get a lot of high-priced call girls trying to work here."

The Winchesters couldn't believe what they were hearing. Sure, they'd been stared at in restaurants, but this man's blatant racism was too much for them.

Mr. Winchester picked up his bags and motioned his wife toward the door. "You'll be hearing from our attorneys," he said quietly to the clerk.

For the Winchesters and other interracial couples, remarks or assumptions about their race often seem surprisingly out of place in this decade. These couples may live in integrated neighborhoods, work with people of all races and know many other interracial couples. Cultural diversity is simply a fact of life for them, whether it's in their marriage or in any other part of their lives.

Negative assumptions about their relationships, like those of the hotel clerk, can be unexpected and espe-

Some interracial couples say that they've been treated poorly in hospitals.

Many interracial couples have strong marriages and wonderful families.

cially harsh. Yet other interracial couples have reported hearing such remarks occasionally, whether it's at an expensive restaurant or an amusement park.

As the number of interracial marriages grows, it is hoped that society's acceptance of them will also grow. The more people see and meet interracial couples, the less likely they will be to think that the marriage is unusual. In 1988, 1.8 percent of all marriages in this country—totaling 956,000—were interracial. In 1970, that number was only .7 percent of all marriages.

Most of the interracial marriages in 1988— 149,000—were between a black man and a white woman. But interracial marriages also include many other races. Tim, a white man, and Tomoko, his Asian wife, have been married for 11 years. They believe they have a strong marriage, as well as supportive friends and family. But they say that they too have had rude remarks and strange looks directed at them. "Some people just can't accept anything that seems out of the ordinary," says Tim.

Tim and Tomoko say their biggest concern is teaching their children to be accepting of others. At the same time, they want their children to learn how to deal with any rude remarks they might receive. As parents, Tim and Tomoko say they have learned how important it is for children to feel that they fit in with their peers.

"WHAT ARE YOU, ANYWAY?"

Krista picked up her lunch tray and turned to look over the cafeteria. Scanning the tables, she finally spotted the group of girls she had been looking for. Whew, she thought with relief. She really didn't want to eat alone.

It had been hard enough to be the "new kid at school." Eleven-year-old Krista had struggled to make friends with the kids in her class. It wasn't easy. The kids here weren't mean, just different. At her old school, everyone knew her and she knew everyone. She had never gotten the curious looks from kids that she was getting here.

But it was getting better, thought Krista as she headed for the table. At least this group of girls had been friendly and open.

"Hi!" she said, sitting down.

The four girls stared at Krista, then looked at one another. Finally, one of them said quickly, "Hi, Krista."

Krista studied their faces. What's up? she thought. Usually they were talking and laughing and teasing one another. Now there was an awkward silence as each of them concentrated on their food between quick glances at Krista.

Suddenly, one of them, Sherise, said, "So, Krista, you didn't tell us you were such *good* friends with Lisa and Heather. Are you hanging out with them now, or what?"

"Oh, you mean the two girls in my science class?" Krista said. "I just talked to them before school this morning. We weren't really hanging out," she finished, a little confused. "Don't you like Lisa and Heather?" she asked Sherise.

Sherise put down her sandwich and looked straight at Krista. "Are you blind or something?" she said. "Do you see them sitting with us? I don't think so. They don't really want to be friends with anybody who's African American—including us."

Krista stared back at Sherise in surprise. "What?"

Another girl, Diane, spoke up. "They smile at us and say hi. But they never want to sit next to us in class or talk to us. So we don't hang out with them or their white friends."

"They probably only talked to you because you're light-skinned," said Sherise. "I bet they don't even know that you're black. Are your parents light?"

Krista laughed. "Well, I guess you could say that. My mom is white."

The four girls all stared at Krista. "Really?" said Diane under her breath. "So what are you—black or white?"

Krista shrugged. "I'm not either." She looked around at her friends. What did it matter?

Children of interracial marriages may have a hard time fitting in with peer groups.

Sherise pushed her chair back. "Well, I think you better decide. Because if you're gonna hang out with Lisa and Heather, you can't hang out with us. Right?"

Krista sat back in shock. She couldn't believe she was being asked to choose.

Krista is not alone in her confusion. We are often asked to identify our race for school, on applications or on official government forms. A child of parents of different races is thus asked to decide between one race and the other.

People are often asked to identify their race in school or on applications. This can be difficult for people with mixed ethnic backgrounds.

A few decades ago, some of these children were accused of trying to "pass" as whites. These people, who were light-skinned, sometimes said that passing as white helped them to get jobs and better treatment by a society that was biased against people of African-American ancestry. Passing angered some blacks, who felt that these people should be proud of their black heritage. They felt that passing further weakened efforts to achieve equality.

Other children wanted to be considered black. Some of them felt that the black community was open and accepting of them, while the white community rejected them. Some said that their skin coloring made them targets of discrimination. They felt that the black community was better able to understand their anger.

Today, many *biracial* children—those with parents of two different races—say that they have been able to identify with both of their parents' cultures. Their parents often have friends from a variety of cultures, and the children say that they too have a culturally mixed group of friends. In fact, many interracial couples say that worries about the children are just another excuse for disapproving of mixed relationships.

BRANDON'S STORY

Today, on a few high school and college campuses, support groups for the children of mixed marriages are springing up. In these groups, people share their experiences. They help one another cope with the problems they face in a society not always willing to accept them.

"My parents were very understanding," Brandon said. "They knew how hard high school was for me, since I was always choosing between two groups of friends. Their attention and caring helped ease some of my more difficult problems."

For 21-year-old Brandon Ellison, the choice of friends, interests and cultures only got more difficult as he finished high school and went on to college.

"At high school, I made a number of black friends and became very interested in African-American culture. Before that, my white mother had always been the one to take great interest in my schoolwork. But suddenly I felt as if I had to hide Mom from my African-American friends. I didn't think she would be interested or understand my wanting to know more about my black heritage. I felt bad shutting her out, but she wasn't part of my black culture, or so I thought."

Fortunately, Brandon's parents sensed his uneasiness. When his mother noticed that he wasn't talking to her about his schoolwork anymore, she had a talk with her

Support groups can help people with mixed ethnic backgrounds deal with the hardships they face.

son. They both felt that the discussion was very helpful. They agreed to discuss anything having to do with Brandon's interracial background. Brandon's mother also emphasized that it was all right for him to have interests of his own. And that, said Brandon, made him begin to feel like his own person, one who was welcome in both worlds.

But, as Brandon told his support group, other problems arose when he went away to college. "Hundreds of miles from home, I again felt lonely and caught between two worlds. Even choosing a dormitory to live in was a problem. The white and black groups on campus seemed to want to have nothing to do with each other. Few people were sensitive to my situation. I either had to be black or white. It was Guns 'n' Roses or Bobby

Brown, but not both. No one understood that my heritage involved many different interests. I was alone again. That is, until this group formed. Sharing my diverse interests and concerns—just like I did with my parents—has definitely changed my college experience for the better."

"WHAT ABOUT *OUR* CULTURE?"

Like other interracial couples, George and Susan Thompson had faced many problems. They had dealt with housing discrimination and the curses and dirty looks from members of both races. But their love for each other kept their marriage strong and happy. Despite some difficulties with George's parents, the newlyweds felt on top of the world. When their first child, Jarad, was born, the Thompsons were thrilled.

Gradually, however, the problems with George's parents grew worse. Ellis and Arlene Thompson continually reminded George to remember his African roots. They pushed George to teach the now eight-year-old Jarad about his Muslim heritage. Their grandson, they said, wasn't going to be an *Uncle Tom.* "We didn't fight for equality for hundreds of years so you could deny your culture," said George's father.

It's important for people of all ages and ethnic backgrounds to feel comfortable with who they are.

George's parents' attitude caused much anger and sadness for George and Susan. They had agreed to try to explain both their cultures and religions to Jarad. But now, George's parents continually ignored or put down Susan's Christian faith. Whenever Jarad was with Grandma and Grandpa Thompson, he would learn only about one faith and one heritage.

The attitudes toward interracial marriage expressed by George's parents are held by other African Americans as well. They feel that African Americans need to keep their faith and culture from being forgotten or purposely neglected by a dominant white culture. They may worry that so many years of struggling to have their voices heard will be lost unless future generations learn about and continue that struggle. If Jarad and other children try to maintain two cultures, George's parents and others like them feel that one or both of those cultures are bound to suffer.

EVELYN AND ART

For some couples, issues about raising children and mixing cultures seem very remote. These couples may find that simply getting married poses problems they never anticipated.

Evelyn and Art have been dating for four years. About six months ago, they decided to get married.

Because Art had been a member of a community church for a long time, the couple wanted to be married in that church. They immediately visited the pastor of that church to ask him to perform the service. Art's parents were happy and excited that Art and Evelyn would be married by a familiar face.

But it turned out that the pastor was not so happy. When he met with Art and Evelyn, he didn't try to hide his uneasiness about marrying an interracial couple. Art and Evelyn were stunned. No one had ever made an issue of the fact that Art is white and Evelyn is Haitian-American before, and they certainly did not expect to encounter discrimination from the church.

"What difference does our color make?" Art asked angrily. "Doesn't the church accept both of us?"

The pastor smiled. "I'm sure that you're both fine people," he said. "But this is a personal decision. I just don't believe that this marriage can be the will of God."

For Art and Evelyn and for Art's parents, the pastor's decision came as a shock. Art's parents felt that they had always taught their children not to discriminate, and they were sure that their church supported this teaching. But now the pastor they had trusted for years was refusing to recognize the most important decision in their son's life. Like Art and Evelyn, they felt angry and betrayed.

Many religious leaders welcome interracial couples into their congregations and perform their marriages. But there are some, like Art's pastor, who believe that mixed marriages are wrong. Though an organized church may officially have a policy against discrimination, a pastor may act on his or her own in refusing to marry a couple. Some say that such a marriage, especially between black and white, is condemned by Biblical teachings. Others, of course, think that this claim is ridiculous.

Art and Evelyn simply found another pastor who was happy to marry the couple. This pastor also told them about different support groups across the country for interracial couples. These groups share newsletters and stories and provide information and assistance for couples with questions or problems.

In the past, some people felt that interracial couples faced an increased chance of getting divorced. They thought that an interracial marriage would face added pressure from families or the community. Adding society's racial tensions to the already difficult job of keeping a marriage together would just be too much, many thought.

But today, many experts say that no solid evidence has shown that the divorce rate increases for interracial couples. Couples like Art and Evelyn should try to share cultural differences and discuss potential problems as any married couple should.

Today, as interracial marriages continue to increase, they continue to provide mixed reactions from society. Some people believe that these marriages are no different from other marriages. But others feel uncomfortable with the idea of racial mixing. Most interracial couples know that their marriage may seem unusual or controversial to some. But they hope their openness and willingness to talk about their marriages will help others to better understand these very personal relationships.

FOR MORE INFORMATION

For more information about interracial marriage, you can visit your local library or community cultural centers. The American Association for Marriage and Family Therapy in Washington, D.C. offers referrals to local agencies. You can contact them at (202) 452-0109.

GLOSSARY/INDEX

BIRACIAL 37—*Consisting of two races.*

CIVIL RIGHTS MOVEMENT 10, 15, 16, 17—*A series of protests and legal changes aimed at improving the status of minorities in the United States.*

DESEGREGATION 17—*The practice of eliminating the separation of one racial group from others.*

KU KLUX KLAN 16—*A group of whites that believe in the separation of the races.*

MISCEGENATION 9, 10, 12—*Mixing of the races.*

MIXED MARRIAGE 15, 38, 44—*Another word used to describe a marriage between people of different races or religions.*

MULATTO 10—*A first-generation offspring of a black and a white.*

OCTOROON 10—*A word used to describe a person of one-eighth black ancestry.*

QUADROON 10—*A word used to describe a person of one-fourth black ancestry.*

UNCLE TOM 40—*A black who is subservient to whites.*